Frantic Assembly presents

Hymns

By Chris O'Connell

Original production commissioned by the
Gantry, Southampton Arts Centre
Originally produced in association with the
Lyric Hammersmith

Hymns

By Chris O'Connell

Hymns was first performed at The Drum Theatre, Plymouth on 14 September 1999, with the following cast:

Scott Graham
Steven Hoggett
Simon Rees
Karl Sullivan

It was remounted in spring 2005 with the following tour:

22–26 February	Contact Theatre, Manchester
1–3 March	Theatre Royal, Winchester
4–5 March	The Gardner Arts Centre, Brighton
9–12 March	Warwick Arts Centre, Coventry
15–19 March	West Yorkshire Playhouse, Leeds
14–16 April	Everyman Theatre, Liverpool
19 April – 7 May	Lyric Hammersmith, London

Cast

Scott	**Steven Hoggett**
Steven	**Eddie Kay**
Karl	**Karl Sullivan**
Simon	**Joseph Traynor**

Written by	**Chris O'Connell**
Director and Choreographer	**Liam Steel**
Co-directors	**Scott Graham** and **Steven Hoggett**
Lighting Design	**Natasha Chivers**
Production Manager	**Richard Eustace**
Company Stage Manager	**Joni Carter**
Technical Stage Manager	**Paul Lim**
Soundtrack	**Steven Hoggett, DJ Andy Cleeton, Liam Steel**
General Manager	**Gordon Millar**
Administrator	**Sinead Mac Manus**
Company Associate	**Vicki Middleton**
Production Runners	**Trudy Bell Chloe Layla Osborne**
PR/Company Associate	**Ben Chamberlain Chamberlain AMPR**
Marketing Manager	**Clair Chamberlain Chamberlain AMPR**
Graphic Design	**Emma Cooke Stem Design**

Frantic Assembly would like to thank: Vicky Featherstone, Simon Mellor and Ben Chamberlain. Thanks also to Jonathon Clark and Simon Sturgess for work on the original *Hymns* production. Love to Sian Graham and Marco Favoro. Special thanks to Karl Sullivan. *Hymns* 05 is dedicated to Vicki Middleton, the memory of Nick Bourne and the arrival of Marcia Graham.

Biographies

Steven Hoggett Performer and Co-director

Steven is co-founder and Artistic Director with Frantic Assembly. Director/ performer credits for Frantic include *Look Back in Anger, Klub, Flesh, Zero, Sell Out, Hymns* (original production), *Heavenly, Tiny Dynamite* (co-production with Paines Plough) and *On Blindness* (co-production with Paines Plough and Graeae). Directorial credits include *Underworld*, *Peepshow* and *Rabbit* for Frantic, *Service Charge* (Lyric Hammersmith) and *Air* (MAC, Birmingham). Co-direction and choreography credits include *Vs.* (Karim Tonsi Dance Company, Cairo), *Waving* (Oily Carte), *Improper* (Bare Bones Dance Company), *Subterrain* (Farm Productions) and *The Straits* (Paines Plough). Additional performance credits include *Manifesto* (Volcano Theatre Company), *Go Las Vegas* (The Featherstonehaughs) and *Outside Now* for Prada (Milan Fashion Week 2001).

Eddie Kay Performer

Eddie studied at Northern School of Contemporary Dance in the early 90s. After which he went on to work with Lois Taylor of Attik Dance Co, teaching and performing in rural parts of SW England. Joining DV8 in 2000, he travelled to Australia with *The Cost of Living* as part of the Sydney Olympic Arts Festival. This piece was then redeveloped in 2003 for an installation at TATE Modern, London and in the same year was made into a film for Channel Four. Over the last few years Eddie has been living in Australia, teaching and performing for companies such as Legs on the Wall, Igneous and Big man wee Man. As well as teaching at Queensland University of Technology he has taught extensively throughout Victoria and New South Wales. Although he admits to learning much on his travels, nothing has yet come close to what he has shared and observed on the dance floor at his parents' parties.

Karl Sullivan Performer

Karl joined Frantic for the original production of *Hymns*. More recently he has played Driver in *Rabbit* and ensemble roles the Royal National Theatre's *Cyrano de Bergerac*, Hamlet's Ghost and Dostoevsky's Idiot for Arc Dance Company. Karl has worked for several other contemporary dance companies in the UK and Ireland including Adventures in Motion Pictures, V-tol Dance Company and Irish Modern Dance Theatre. Karl is also a choreographer and workshop leader/movement teacher.

Joseph Traynor Performer

Theatre credits include *Taylor's Dummies* (Gecko), *The Boy Who Left Home* (ATC), *De La Guarda* (De La Guarda), *Rats Bucket and Bombs* (Nottingham Playhouse), *Salomie* (Royal National Theatre Studio and Gate), *Cleaning* (One Tree Company) and *Bed Show* (Bristol Old Vic Studio). TV credits include *The Iceman Murder, Doctors*, *Chambers* and *Dickens*. Film credits include *4am*.

Chris O'Connell Writer

After winning a Pearson Television Theatre Writers Bursary, Chris was Writer-in-Residence for Paines Plough, 1999–2000. Plays for Theatre Absolute include: *Car*, *Raw* and *Kid*, *Big Burger Chronicles*, and *She's Electric*. *Car* and *Raw* won Fringe Firsts at the Edinburgh Festival, (99, 01), and *Car* won a Time Out Live Award, 1999, Best Play on the Fringe. Other recent work by Chris includes: *Tall Phoenix* (Belgrade Theatre), *Thyestes* (RSC), *Hold Ya'* (Red Ladder Theatre Co), *Auto* (Vanemuine Theatre, Estonia), *Southwark* (Paines Plough), *Cool Water Murder* (Belgrade Theatre), *The Blue Zone* (mac Productions) and *Gabriel's Ashes* for BBC Radio 4. His work has been both read and produced in Estonia, Italy, Australia and America. Chris is currently Playwright in Residence at Birmingham University, attached to their M(Phil) in playwrighting.

Liam Steel Director

In addition to working as a freelance director, choreographer and performer, Liam is artistic director of his own company 'Stan Won't Dance' which toured its first piece *Sinner* through 2004 to critical acclaim. For eight years he was a core member of DV8 Physical Theatre as both a performer and Assistant Director of the company. Productions worked on included *MSM; Enter Achilles* (including the Emmy award winning film version); *Bound to Please; The Happiest Day of My Life;* and *The Cost of Living*. His previous involvement with Frantic includes directing and choreographing the original production of *Hymns*; choreographing, co-directing and performing in the British tour and off-Broadway productions of *Heavenly*, and co-devising and performing in the BAC scratch production. Other freelance performance credits include work with Complicité; Nottingham Playhouse; The Royal Court; Manchester Royal Exchange; The Kosh; Volcano Theatre Co; Roundabout Theatre Co; Gay Sweatshop; Theatr Powys; Footloose Dance Company (Powys Dance); Nigel Charnock and Company; Theatre Centre; Royal National Theatre Studio; Graeae Theatre Co; and David Glass Ensemble. Directorial/choreographic work includes *The Shooky,* (Birmingham Repertory Theatre); *Paradise Lost (*Northampton Theatre Royal); *Pericles* (RSC/Cardboard Citizens Theatre Co); *Devotion (*Theatre Centre); *Frankenstein* (Blue Eyed Soul Dance Company); *Vurt* (Contact Theatre, Manchester); *The Fall of the House of Usher* (Graeae Theatre Company); *Look at Me, (*Theatre Centre); *Sparkleshark*, (Royal National Theatre); *The Flight* (Restless Dance Co. (Adelaide Festival-Australia)); *15 Degrees and Rising* (The Circus Space); *The Secret Garden*; *Beauty and the Beast; Tom's Midnight Garden, The Ghosts of Scrooge* (Library Theatre, Manchester); and as choreographer on Tamasha Theatre Company's production of *Strictly Dandia* for which he was awarded a Herald Angel for Outstanding Achievement at the 2003 Edinburgh International Festival.

Scott Graham Co-director

Scott is co-founder and Artistic Director with Frantic Assembly. Director/ performer credits for Frantic include *Look Back In Anger*, *Klub*, *Flesh*, *Zero*, *Sell Out*, *Hymns* (original production), *Heavenly*, *Tiny Dynamite* (co-production with Paines Plough) and *On Blindness* (co-production with Paines Plough and Graeae). Directorial credits include *Underworld*,

Peepshow and *Rabbit* for Frantic, *Service Charge* (Lyric Theatre, Hammersmith) and *Air* (MAC, Birmingham). Co-direction and choreography credits include *Vs.* (Karim Tonsi Dance Company, Cairo) and *Improper* (Bare Bones Dance Company). Additional performance credits include *Outside Now* for Prada (Milan Fashion week 2001).

Natasha Chivers Lighting Design

Natasha's recent theatre work includes: *Mercury Fur* (Paines Plough/ Plymouth Drum*), Small Thing*s (Paines Plough at The Chocolate Factory), *Pyrenees* (Paines Plough/Tron Theatre Glasgow*), Urban Legend* and *The Kindness Of Strangers* (Liverpool Everyman 40th anniversary Season), *Who's Afraid Of Virginia Woolf, Ma Rainey's Black Bottom* and *The Entertainer* (Liverpool Playhouse); *Who's Afraid Of The Big Bad Book* (Soho Theatre); *The Straits* (59 East 59, New York – Paines Plough, Hampstead Theatre); *Very Little Women* (Lip Service tour); *On Blindness* (Paines Plough, Frantic Assembly, Graeae). Other work includes: *The Cherry Orchard* and *After The Dance* (Oxford Stage Company – tour); *The Bomb-itty of Errors* (The New Ambassadors/Dublin), *Playhouse Creatures* (West Yorkshire Playhouse); *Peepshow* (Frantic Assembly, Plymouth Theatre Royal, Lyric Hammersmith and tour); Sell Out (Frantic Assembly – National and International tours/New Ambassadors Theatre), *Wit* and *The Memory Of Water* (Stellar Quines, Tron, Traverse and tour); *Present Laughter* (Bath Theatre Royal Productions); *The Drowned World* (Paines Plough, Traverse Theatre and Bush Theatre); *Tiny Dynamite* (Frantic Assembly, Paines Plough, Lyric Hammersmith and tour).

Richard Eustace Production Manager

Richard has been a Production Manager for the last seven years working full time at The Gate Theatre and Theatre Royal Stratford East. As a Freelance Production Manager he has worked for Tamasha Theatre Company, ROH2, Stanhope Productions and PW Prods in the West End, the Young Vic, Druid Theatre Company in Ireland, Strathcona Theatre Company, The Clod Ensemble, Theatre Pur, Primitive Science and The Space Project. This is Richard's first job with Frantic Assembly.

Paul Lim Technical Stage Manager

Paul is on loan from Australia where he began his theatrical career. He has over 8 years experience in technical theatre including Lighting Design, Sound Design, Stage and Production Management. Most recently he was Sound Operator for *Jungle Book* at The Old Rep, Birmingham, and on tour with *Tom's Midnight Garden*, and a Stage Manager for Pleasance at Edinburgh Festival Fringe 2004. Paul is a freelance technician based in London.

Joni Carter Company Stage Manager

Joni Carter works as a freelance stage manager, with a keen interest in devised theatre and site-specific pieces. She was company stage manager with Theatre O, touring internationally to festivals with *Three Dark Tales* and *The Argument*. Joni has also project-managed live events and installations at the Tate Modern and the Royal Festival Hall. Most recently Joni has worked with Unicorn Theatre and Shakespeare's International Globe.

frantic assembly

Renowned both nationally and internationally for attracting new, young audiences, Frantic Assembly stand at the forefront of modern British physical theatre. Over the past ten years Frantic has established itself as one of the most pioneering and exciting companies around, touring extensively throughout the UK including a ground-breaking West End run in 1999. Six-time recipients of *Time Out Critics Choice*, the company also received a *Time Out Live Award* for *Sell Out* in 1998. To date, Frantic have presented their work in almost 30 countries worldwide, and are studied in schools and universities throughout Britain.

The key to this success lies with the intention and nature of the work. Frantic produces intelligent, relevant theatre, which engages, excites and energises audiences with a style firmly rooted in contemporary culture. The themes of the work are drawn from everyday life, attitudes and practices. The intention is to bring about an understanding of people's experience, behaviour and environment, in a way that is accessible and stimulating.

Future projects include *Dirty Wonderland* – a site-specific project performed in a hotel for the Brighton Festival.

Frantic Assembly are:

Artistic Director	Scott Graham
Artistic Director	Steven Hoggett
General Manager	Gordon Millar
Administrator	Sinead Mac Manus
Associates	Ben Chamberlain and Vicki Middleton
Advisory Board	Vicky Featherstone and Simon Mellor

Frantic Assembly
BAC, Lavender Hill
London SW11 5TN
Tel: 020 7228 8885 / Fax: 020 7738 2225
admin@franticassembly.co.uk
www.franticassembly.co.uk

The free resource pack, *A Teacher's Guide to* Hymns, workshops and INSET training days are available to schools. For more details visit www.franticassembly.co.uk.

Friends Scheme
To mark our 10th Anniversary Frantic Assembly has set up a Friends scheme. By becoming a **Frantic Friend** or **Assembly Associate** you will support our continued commitment to excellence in both our **productions** and **education policy**. There are also plenty of benefits for you. To find out more or to join visit www.franticassembly.co.uk.

Frantic Assembly are supported by

The Lyric Hammersmith presents some of the most original theatre to be found in London. As well as the productions we make ourselves, we work with some of the most exciting theatre companies in Britain and abroad.

This Spring we welcome the Young Vic with their acclaimed production *A Raisin in the Sun*; Tamasha Theatre Company with their 2004 sell-out success *Strictly Dandia*; and we have the world premiere of *Some Girls Are Bigger Than Others* from Anonymous Society with the songs of Morrissey and Marr.

We are delighted that Frantic Assembly are back at the Lyric to celebrate their 10th anniversary with this landmark production. *Hymns* was first seen at the Lyric in 1999.

We hope you enjoy the show.

For more information about the Lyric Hammersmith visit **www.lyric.co.uk**

We are always pleased to hear from members of our audience. If you have any comments or suggestions please write to:

Simon Mellor, Executive Director
Lyric Hammersmith
Lyric Square
London W6 0QL

Artistic Directors' Note

Frantic Assembly's 10th anniversary comes as a result of many things. A love of bruises, a desire to discover just what else theatre might be, an open mind and a flagrant disregard for one's bank balance are just a few of the factors we remember.

Anniversaries often become opportunities for reflection and in our case we asked ourselves whether we had any unfinished business regarding the Frantic back catalogue. Our decision to revisit *Hymns* comes after realising there was more to be found from the subject matter of the original production, both physically and textually. Working again with Chris O'Connell has been an incredibly vitalising experience, realising that as thinking and opinionated individuals we are different to the same team of only five years ago. It is fascinating to discover how experience, both collective and singular, already compels us to present truth on stage in a different way. It also confirms that, in looking to the issues covered in *Hymns*, we were more than just timely, as the questions raised then are still as pertinent. The project also allows us to further our working relationship with Liam Steel who remains as inspirational to us now as on the first day we met him. His vision and demands on our company have been truly formative and it has only been his shirt collection that has ever proved as challenging.

Hymns also stands as the most requested Frantic show and several years after the tour finished, the Frantic office was still receiving regular calls and e mails asking if there were any plans to re-tour the piece. To truly stand by our commitment in providing the best contemporary work we possibly can, it is important to respond to this kind of request. And so it is with a newly inspired company that we are able to present this existing work and in doing so, allow a brand new audience to discover what we were banging on about way back when we had no idea what it might mean to wear a harness back to front every night for an eight month tour.

The tour also marks the introduction of two new Frantic members – Eddie Kay and Joseph Traynor. Performers like these two are hard to find and we thank them in advance for agreeing to a rehearsal process and subsequent tour which sees the return of the aforementioned harnesses. Long may you chafe....

Frantic today would be nothing without a decade of love, sweat and tears. The very working dynamic of the company has always meant that it was essential we find artists of the highest quality and with the most generous spirit.

To this end, we consider ourselves truly blessed looking back over the people who have gone to make up the Frantic Assembly since we first started. It is purely this that has allowed an unknown and unknowing Swansea collective to experience a working life that takes in everything from the rural valleys of Wales to the Sahara desert, Hungarian bath houses to Taiwanese hot-tubs, from the back of a fume-filled transit van to the West End of London in ten quick years.

Frantic life has been a beautiful time and you Frantic boys and girls out there are truly wonderful.

Scott Graham and Steven Hoggett
January 2005

writer's note

Remembering when Frantic Assembly first commissioned me to write *Hymns* always makes me smile, because having seen their previous work I was perplexed, to say the least, as to how I could write a play for four ridiculously fit guys who were going to throw themselves around a stage. Well okay, I could imagine some words, but where in the 'play' would they do their 'dancy bits'? What I managed to come up with back then quickly took shape in the rehearsal room, and now as we've returned to it, the play has become the piece that is published in this text. It was brought together in a fantastically collaborative way which speaks volumes for the vision of the company, and how they imagine their theatre.

Hymns leaves me richer in the belief that physicality and words can live *equally* alongside each other, with narrative valued as strongly as the 'dancy bits'! I feel most proud of it in those spine-tingling moments when through the softest touch or the most visceral surge of energy, words suddenly become movements, and movements turn back into words.

There's no attempt in the text to define or notate any of the physical/dance sequences; they are what they are, and they can't be described, least of all by someone who can only pogo.

Chris O'Connell
January 2005

HYMNS

First published in 2005 by Oberon Books Ltd
521 Caledonian Road, London N7 9RH
Tel: 020 7607 3637 / Fax: 020 7607 3629
e-mail: oberon.books@btinternet.com
www.oberonbooks.com

This production has been licensed by arrangement with The
Agency (London) Ltd, 24 Pottery Lane, London W11 4LZ,
email: info@theagency.co.uk.

A catalogue record for this book is available from the British
Library.

ISBN: 1 84002 548 4

Cover image by Emma Cooke at Stem Design.

Printed in Great Britain by Antony Rowe Ltd, Chippenham.

Characters

SCOTT

STEVEN

SIMON

KARL

At the time of publication this play was still in rehearsal and there may be some differences between what is on the page, and what is on the stage.

1

SCOTT, STEVEN, SIMON and KARL. All are on stage.

A funeral. Voice over is heard:

SIMON: Which chapel are we in?

STEVEN: Look on the list. And make sure we get the right one.

SCOTT: Jesus, don't get us in the wrong chapel.

SIMON: Steve, what chapel is it in?

STEVEN: How would I know?

SIMON: Are you alright?

KARL: Yeah, I'll be fine.

SIMON: Are you sure?

KARL: Yes.

Extracts from Psalm 23 are heard.

I can't believe we're doing this.

STEVEN: It'll be fine. (*Beat.*) It'll be fine.

SIMON: It doesn't seem fair.

SCOTT: It never is.

The Psalm is heard again.

ALL: Amen.

STEVEN: It'll be fine.

Pause.

Good turn out.

KARL: I didn't know he knew so many people.

SCOTT: Nor did he.

A mobile phone goes off.

STEVEN: It'll be fine.

SCOTT answers his mobile.

SCOTT: (*Mobile.*) Hello?… Hi… Jesus, I thought I'd turned the thing off… Yeah? What? I don't know, did you look in the tray by my desk…not there…? What about the black filing cabinet, it should be in the black filing cabinet… Yeah? Have a look…

STEVEN: Scott.

SCOTT: (*Mobile.*) Ring me if you can't find it… Yeah, I'm alright, well I'm at a funeral…what about you…?… Did he? Really…? Sounds great, yeah yeah, look I better get going. In a couple of days, I'll see you then…alright…thanks for calling…

SCOTT joins the other three who've waited for him to finish.

Sorry about that guys.

KARL raises his bottle

KARL: A toast. To Jimi.

As they clink bottles, music plays and a physical sequence begins.

SCOTT: What's orange and blue and lies at the bottom of the ocean?
A baby with duff armbands.

KARL: Why do dogs lick their bollocks?
Because they can.

SIMON: What's got two legs and bleeds?
Half a dog.

SCOTT: What do you call a man with a rabbit up his arse?

ALL: Warren.

STEVEN: What do you call an Essex girl in a white shell suit?
The bride.

SIMON: What do you call a man with no shins?
Neil.

STEVEN: What do you call an epileptic in a paper bag?

KARL: Russell. What did the leper say to the prostitute?
Keep the tip.

STEVEN: What's blue and mugs old ladies?
Hypothermia.

SIMON: What do you call a Russian prostitute?
Knickersonandoffski.

STEVEN/SIMON: What do you get if you cross a dyslexic agnostic with an insomniac?

SCOTT/KARL: Someone who lies awake at night wondering if there's a dog.

KARL: What do you call a pig with three eyes?
Piiig.

SCOTT: (*To STEVEN.*) Ten more minutes and then I'm going.

STEVEN: What's the biggest draw back in the jungle?

SCOTT: An elephant's foreskin.

STEVEN: (*To SCOTT.*) Stay for a bit.

KARL: What do you call a woman with no legs?

SIMON: (*To SCOTT.*) I feel weird.

KARL: Fanny Walker.

SCOTT: (*To SIMON.*) You've always been weird.

STEVEN: What's the difference between a lesbian and a walrus?
One's fat and hairy and stinks of fish; the other's a walrus.

SCOTT: (*To STEVEN.*) Ten more minutes and then I'm going.

SIMON: Does anyone want another drink?

OTHERS: Got one thanks.

SIMON: What's brown, and sticky?
A stick.

STEVEN: (*To SCOTT.*) How long are you up for?

SCOTT: I told you earlier.

STEVEN: Forgot.

SCOTT: Two days. (*Beat. To SIMON and KARL.*) Hey, dig the suits!

SIMON: Really?

SCOTT: No, they're fucking awful.

STEVEN: Why did the Mexican push his wife off a cliff?

KARL: (*To SCOTT.*) You managed to get the day off then.

SIMON: Tequila.

SCOTT: Yeah. So what're we doing then?

STEVEN: What?

SCOTT: Well we don't have to stay here, not now it's all over.

STEVEN: What do you mean?

SCOTT: We could go somewhere.

SIMON: It didn't last long.

SCOTT: What?

SIMON: The day.

SCOTT: Go somewhere, find a club, find a bar, have a lap dance, I'm not that fussed, maybe go for a curry...all night garage...bus shelter...

STEVEN: Scott, just...

SCOTT: What?

KARL holds his bottle up as before.

KARL: A toast. To Jimi.

ALL: To Jimi.

2

Music plays. Until...

SCOTT: Guys, you can loosen up a bit, yeah? No one's going to report you.

SIMON: He had them all talking, they were all saying what a brilliant guy he was.

SCOTT: You sure they were talking about the same person?

SIMON: Best funeral I've ever been to.

SCOTT: It's the only funeral you've ever been to.

SIMON: I was wondering what you'd all be doing if it was mine, probably all have gone home.

SCOTT: Probably wouldn't have come.

STEVEN: What would you go for: burial, or cremation?

SIMON: Burial.

SCOTT: Cremation. I quite like that urn they put Jimi in. Very retro.

SIMON: How do you know you've got the right urn at the end of it, is there a form you sign or something?

SCOTT: Probably got someone behind the curtain... (*Laughing.*) Yeah, they've got this checkout girl on New Deal, she looks after it all, makes sure the conveyer belt doesn't get stuck, pings the bar code on the coffin as it goes through... Sorry, this one hasn't got a price on it, he'll have to wait. Jason, can you find a price for this corpse?… (*As Jason.*) Aisle 3… Aisle 3… (*To STEVEN and SIMON.*)…another name for a corpse…quick…

STEVEN: Cadaver.

SCOTT: Nice…stick with it, (*Headline.*) "Scott takes Checkout girl scenario to hilarious conclusion…"

SIMON: He hopes.

SCOTT: He will… (*As Jason.*) "Aisle 3: Cadavers. £25.50" (*As Checkout girl.*) "Thanks Jase…" And then super checkout girl's turning the gas on, (*Makes blazing fire noise.*) Phrrrggggh! Fuck's sake, is that a bit hot?…

STEVEN: She always burns the toast at home.

SCOTT: (*Laughing.*) Yeah… Phrrrgghh! Blast! Coffin disintegrates, music plays, she scoops the ashes up, gives them a shake and bam! into the urn, label it up, wait for the mum and dad at the back door. Is this your urn? Number 43. Do you want it wrapped? Hey, sorry, I nearly forgot!…do you want fries with that?

The three of them are laughing.

Marks out of ten.

STEVEN: 7.

SCOTT: 8 at least. (*Beat.*) I was thinking: it's the only 'do' Jimi's been to when he didn't get out of his box.

STEVEN: It's got to be the first time I've ever seen Jimi smoke.

SIMON: I nearly had a coffin fit.

They are laughing again.

KARL: Alright!

Silence.

SIMON: It's just a laugh.

KARL: I know it is.

Silence. They each take a cigarette.

SCOTT: (*To SIMON.*) What were you up to anyway?

SIMON: When?

SCOTT: In the church, chatting up the organist.

STEVEN: Was she giving you lessons on your upright?

SIMON: I was suggesting a hymn I wanted her to play.

SCOTT: 'Kumbaya My Lord.'

STEVEN: 'Jesus Wants Me For A Sunbeam'.

KARL: 'If I Had A Hammer'.

SIMON: No.

SCOTT: 'Come On Baby Light My Fire'.

STEVEN: 'On The Wings of Love'.

SIMON: 'Ghost Town'.

STEVEN and SCOTT look at each other.

SCOTT: If you say so… 'Stairway To Heaven'.

STEVEN: 'Bat Out Of Hell'.

SIMON: 'Love Me Tender'.

Another look from STEVEN to SCOTT; they press on.

SCOTT: 'My Way'.

STEVEN: 'Bright Eyes'.

SCOTT: 'Candle In The Wind'.

STEVEN: 'Lady In Red'.

SCOTT: 'Bridge Over Troubled Water.'

SIMON: 'Little Town of Bethlehem'.

STEVEN: (*To SCOTT.*) He's not playing properly.

SIMON: No, that's what it was.

Pause.

STEVEN: Do you know what fucking month it is?!

SIMON: I like the tune.

SCOTT: It's a fucking *carol…* Why? What the fuck possessed you to ask her to play 'Oh Little Town of Bethlehem'?

SIMON: I wanted to contribute something.

SCOTT: But why a *carol*?

SIMON: Forget it.

SCOTT: I can't, it's etched on my brain. It'll never go away.

Music plays. Physical sequence. Until...

STEVEN: Who was it by the way, who couldn't keep in tune with the rest of us?

KARL: What you looking at me for?

General impressions of a cat's chorus.

I didn't think we'd be singing and shit...never sang in my life before.

SIMON: You thought it'd be a bit of a chat, and then back to the Vicar's for tea.

KARL: Something like that.

SIMON: So you never sang anything, not even at school?

KARL: Probably did some nativity play thing.

SIMON: Who did you play?

SCOTT / STEVEN: Bethlehem!

SIMON: Yeah, yeah, fuck off.

KARL: Jimi was a donkey. (*They all look at him.*) Once, he told me, we were pissed...he was a donkey at his school and he had big stick up ears his old lady made for him, fluffy tail and a pink nose he put on with lipstick.

Pause. They press on...

STEVEN: Shit, I just remembered!

SIMON: What?

STEVEN: Jimi owed me a tenner the bastard!

Music plays. Physical sequence. Until...

SIMON: Can't get used to it.

SCOTT: It's going to take ages, days, weeks, then you'll realise he's old news.

KARL: It's not like he was someone in the paper.

SCOTT: I know that.

KARL: It was Jimi, we knew him.

SCOTT: Yeah, but it's just what happens. You'll always miss him, but after a while it'll be like you've forgotten him.

SIMON: No.

SCOTT: Yeah, when you're forty, he'll still be twenty-six, you won't've known him for fourteen years.

SIMON: He's our friend.

SCOTT: It doesn't mean I liked him any less. I'd say the same about you. I actually forgot your name earlier, I haven't seen you for six months and I couldn't think if you were Steven or Karl. Just cos we're all mates, it doesn't mean you're in my head all the time. (*Beat.*) I've got other things in my life.

STEVEN: Sure. (*To SIMON.*) He didn't really forget your name.

SCOTT: That was a desperate moment by the way, (*Pulls out his mobile.*) I thought I'd turned the thing off.

STEVEN: Well, you're a busy man.

SCOTT: Couldn't look at you. (*Beat.*) Am I?

STEVEN: I'm guessing. Don't know, are you?

Beat. SCOTT decides to ignore STEVEN

SCOTT: I was surprised I didn't get the old bolt of lightning.

STEVEN: Who says you won't? There's nothing else you feel guilty about is there?

SCOTT: No.

STEVEN: Right. (*Opening it out to the others.*) The mobile was cool anyhow. It doesn't matter if we were laughing, you have to let it out. How many times do you get to do that?

SCOTT: Do what?

STEVEN: Let yourself go, be what you are.

SIMON: That's how I want my funeral to be.

KARL: That's a crock of shit.

SIMON: What is?

SCOTT: Jesus, I love it. I go away for six months and Steve's started talking like he's the PR for the Hippy Foundation, and Karl's walking round with a face like a baboon's arse. What's going on with you lot?

KARL: 'Be what you are'.

SIMON: Karl, we know you're upset alright, we all are, Jimi was a mate.

KARL: (*Of SCOTT.*) He hasn't stopped pissing about since the minute he got off the train.

SCOTT: That's cos I came by car.

STEVEN: (*Of SCOTT.*) He's always pissing about, he's a sarky bastard.

SCOTT: Bless you. (*Beat. To KARL.*) Are you so upset that you can't act civil?

KARL: Like?

SCOTT: Well maybe you can stop sneering at us every time we say something.

KARL: Be what you are.

SIMON: Why're we arguing?

SCOTT: We're mates, we're supposed to argue.

STEVEN: Yeah, but usually when we argue it's about whose round it is, or who's going to win the footie, but now we've got something like this...and it's like we're scared of it, we're acting like it hasn't happened.

SCOTT: Maybe I missed something, but I thought we *were* talking about it.

STEVEN: No...yeah... I've been listening to us, all we've done is take the piss out of each other,

(*Glancing at SCOTT.*) act like we don't care, (*Looking at KARL.*) or like we're martyrs, or something.

KARL: *Fuck off.*

STEVEN: Well we can get it out in the open. All of us. (*Beat.*) Talk about things...

Beat.

SCOTT: You want us to do a 'Tricia' thing?

STEVEN: We could just talk... That's all I'm saying.

3

Music plays. The four of them stand on a table. Physical sequence with text.

SCOTT: Nice big end.

STEVEN: Great big heaving, squelching.

SIMON: Built in air bag.

KARL: CD standard.

STEVEN: Really short skirt with a beautiful.

SCOTT: Metallic finish.

KARL: Lips.

SIMON: Curves to die for.

SCOTT: Alloy wheels.

STEVEN: Great fuel injection.

KARL: Legs right up to her.

STEVEN: Bumpers.

SCOTT: Really well stacked.

STEVEN: Built for sin.

SCOTT: Great big flapping.

SIMON: Set of windscreen wipers.

STEVEN: Really long hair right down to her.

KARL: Adjustable wing mirrors.

SCOTT: Electric windows, come as standard.

SIMON: Cupid lips.

STEVEN: Knees that were just made for carpet burns.

KARL: Hurts like a beast.

STEVEN: You take the A14 to the roundabout, then the B4129 to the right, over the hump backed bridge to the lights, at the T junction take the low road.

KARL: Yeah, I can see what your problem is. Dirty sparks, dodgy firing. Pull up your starter motor, tighten up your belt, grease your pistons.

SIMON: It's all to do with your three phase. You got your alternating current, too much juice.

SCOTT: Swings in from the left, so he heads the ball, hits the bar, comes back, flips it up, scorcher, top left hand corner. Yes.

ALL: Yeah.

STEVEN: You take the A14.

SIMON: It's your three phase.

KARL: Spark plugs.

SCOTT: Missed the bar.

ALL: Yeah.

SCOTT: Scorcher.

STEVEN: Hump back bridge.

KARL: Greasy pistons.

ALL: Yeah.

SIMON: Comes in from the left.

STEVEN: You've got dodgy firing.

KARL: Overload.

SCOTT: Got it.

ALL: Yeah.

KARL: Back to neutral.

SCOTT: Junction.

STEVEN: You should tighten your belt.

SCOTT: Goal.

ALL: Yeah. Yeah. Yeah. Yeah. Yeah. Yeah.

The sequence ends.

4

SCOTT stands on a chair.

SCOTT: (*Fast.*) …a yard of ale!!!!…all the way down!!!… *I* can do it, I know *I* can do it. Si, you have a go, last time you tried you failed. *Failed.* How's it feel Si…

SIMON: I was about 16.

SCOTT: I know, I know, but knowing you can't drink a yard of ale, how have you survived all these years.

KARL: (*To STEVEN.*) What's he on about?

SCOTT: I'm entertaining, we need an entertainer because otherwise we'll all top ourselves. (*Beat. They look at him.*) Sorry. Okay, how about we just get Si *really* pissed and paint a moustache on him and shave off all his pubes, make a real mess. *Everywhere.* Guys! Fun. It's got three letters. F.U.N. It's what we always have, and it's what we should be having *now*. In honour of Jimi. This isn't a funeral, it's a fucking late night phone-in session, it's an autopsy into how sorry we can all look, it's a travesty, a betrayal of the good-time guys that we know we are. (*Pause.*) Deep down.

STEVEN stares at SCOTT.

Is it my imagination, or have you all got a bit depressing to be with?

STEVEN: Simon.

SIMON: What?

STEVEN: You start.

SCOTT: Start what?

STEVEN: Talking.

SCOTT: Si. (*No reply.*) Steve, I'm trying to save us from ourselves. Yeah?

STEVEN: Better out than in though. Eh?

> *STEVEN slaps the chair. SIMON comes and sits on it, and it's leant backwards. STEVEN is behind him. SCOTT and KARL watch.*

SIMON: Don't know… I was in bed.

SCOTT: What was her name?

STEVEN: Sssh!

SIMON: The alarm didn't go off…so I was just…then the phone rang.

STEVEN: What did you say?

SIMON: Don't remember, it's all a bit of a blur. I was crying; most of the day I felt numb.

> *The chair slams forward.*

STEVEN: Scott?

SCOTT: (*Shrugs.*) Dunno.

SIMON: Come on.

SCOTT: I don't know what to say. I don't know what you want.

STEVEN: I just want us all to talk a bit.

SCOTT: Like what?

No answer.

About what?

No answer.

Are you into all that "where were you when 9/11 kicked off, or where were you when Lady Di died…" bollocks. (*SIMON sniggers.*) Shut up. Who cares where I was when I heard about Jimi. He's still dead.

Silence.

I was at work. I was drinking coffee. Kenco Really Rich, two sugars, blue cup, little crack on the rim…

Silence.

There were two guys outside putting down these new yellow lines. I watched them; there was one line with a bit of a kink in it, and I was thinking how you don't ever see that… Then someone comes into the office, she says there's a call from my mate… (*He looks at KARL.*) Can't remember what I said. What did I say?

No answer.

(*To KARL.*) You told me about Jimi, and I just…

KARL: You went quiet.

SCOTT: I felt cold for a minute, I remember that, cold tingling, like pins and needles in my legs.

KARL: You asked me when the funeral was.

SCOTT: Yeah. That's it, that's all I can remember.

Silence.

SIMON: Karl.

No answer.

Your turn Karl.

SCOTT: Leave him.

STEVEN: (*To KARL.*) Where were you when you last saw Jimi?

KARL stares at STEVEN.

KARL: *What?*

STEVEN: All of us. When's the last time we all *saw* him?

SIMON: Together?

STEVEN: Alone.

SCOTT: Why? (*Of KARL.*) Leave him.

STEVEN: I just want us to remember.

A physical sequence begins. We feel that the dialogue during this is more for SCOTT's benefit than for KARL's.

KARL: (*To STEVEN.*) Yeah? (*Pause.*) I was in the kitchen. He was on the stairs. Okay?

STEVEN: And what?

KARL: That's it.

STEVEN: That's all?

KARL: Yeah! What do you want?

STEVEN: Nothing. So you'd…

KARL: I was in the kitchen… He was on the stairs. Fuck's sake.

STEVEN: And that's it?

KARL: Yeah, that's it.

STEVEN: So you were the last person to see him alive?

Beat.

KARL: What?

STEVEN: I'm just thinking, if he was on the stairs, then you must've been the last person to…

SIMON: *That's enough.*

STEVEN: Why?

KARL: Jimi was dead. Alright?… (*Pause.*) He wasn't even what I'd call my best mate…but he sent *me* the text, not you, not Si, not Scott… Why isn't one of you feeling like this?

STEVEN: Like what?

KARL breaks away from the others. STEVEN pursues him. The physical sequence continues.

KARL: I was in the kitchen… He was on the stairs.

STEVEN: Go on.

Physical sequence ends.

SCOTT: Jesus!…we're supposed to be having a laugh together… What're you doing to him?… When was the last time we all sat up drinking and didn't do something stupid? (*Pause.*) What's wrong with you guys?

STEVEN: You've just been away. We're the same mates we've always been.

Beat.

SCOTT: You reckon?

Music plays. Physical sequence. As the sequence ends, SCOTT and STEVEN break apart from the others.

STEVEN: When's the last time you were back?

SCOTT: Dunno. Christmas, Easter. Birthdays.

STEVEN: Yeah? (*Pause.*) Not mine.

SCOTT looks at him.

My birthday. Last month, you missed it.

SCOTT: Yeah.

STEVEN: How's the job?

SCOTT: Brilliant.

STEVEN: You settled in okay down there?

SCOTT: Yeah.

STEVEN: Plenty of dosh?

SCOTT: Are you after a loan?

STEVEN: No.

SCOTT's mobile bleeps. He checks a text, laughs at it. All the time he ignores STEVEN, and STEVEN watches him.

SCOTT: (*Putting the mobile away.*) Anyway, how about you? How's the fruit and veg stall going?

STEVEN: It's not fruit and veg.

SCOTT: I know. 'Memorabilia'. Selling much?

STEVEN: Shit loads.

Pause.

Are you rushing back? Maybe we can see a film, go and have a pint. Are you staying with your folks?

SCOTT: Yeah. Laugh a minute.

STEVEN: Do you ever get tired?

SCOTT: What of?

Beat.

STEVEN: The way you talk.

SCOTT: You mean the way *you* talk. Look, where I am, I've got people pushing me all the time, people after my job, I have to speak like this.

STEVEN: Just be real.

Beat.

It's irritating the fuck out of me.

SCOTT: I'll go then shall I?

STEVEN: Are you still driving the same car?

SCOTT: What?

STEVEN: Scott, your friend's just died. I think you should show some respect.

SCOTT: The mobile was an accident.

STEVEN: I'm not talking about that.

SCOTT: So what *are* you talking about? Are you on drugs? I'll have some of what you're taking, yeah?!

STEVEN: (*Pause.*) Tell me what you're frightened of.

SCOTT: Now you're pissing me off.

STEVEN: Sorry.

SCOTT: I'd forgotten how much you always end up pissing me off.

Beat.

STEVEN: Yeah, well that's me. Sometimes I don't care *who* I piss off.

SCOTT looks at STEVEN.

SIMON is with KARL. Physical sequence.

SIMON: I meant to give you this.

He gives KARL a card in an envelope. KARL opens it.

Everyone's going on about Jimi, but I just thought…

KARL throws it aside.

What're you doing?

KARL: Don't want it.

SIMON: Why not?

KARL: You and your fucking poems.

SIMON: I'm just trying to…/

KARL: Well say it.

SIMON: What?

KARL: Just *say* it.

SIMON goes. STEVEN picks up the card.

STEVEN: (*To KARL.*) He's only trying to make you feel better. That bit in the church…you were alright…it's hard, it's…

KARL: Yeah.

Pause.

STEVEN: Yeah.

5

SIMON takes KARL's hand. He reads his palm.

SIMON: Have you ever had your palm read?

SCOTT: Who's up for a beer?

KARL: Yeah.

SIMON: I met this old woman once, Welsh, we were waiting at a bus stop.

SCOTT: Si?

SIMON: No ta.

STEVEN: What're you doing?

KARL: He's reading my palm.

SIMON: No.

KARL: You're not reading it?

SIMON: No. I was just going to tell you about that woman.

SCOTT: Old Welsh bird. Standing at a bus stop. How did I know that?

SIMON: You heard me tell him. (*Back to KARL.*) She mapped out my life for me. We're standing there waiting for this bus into town, and she tells me...

Physical sequence begins.

SCOTT: No. 42?

SIMON: What?

SCOTT: No. 42 bus?

SIMON: I don't know what it was.

SCOTT: You don't know what bus you were catching, how were you ever going to get home?

SIMON: Fuck off. (*To KARL.*) She says I'll never achieve the things I'm dreaming about. She starts telling me about my future…

KARL: Your fuscia?

SCOTT: So you were in a garden?

STEVEN: Bus stop. Pay attention.

SIMON: *Future*…my future. Earlier, I was thinking about Jimi, how his life's over, and how my life, our lives are still… See the lines on my hand…

KARL: Which?

SCOTT: He's only got two.

SIMON: Fucking hell…everything's there, no gaps, no uncertainties…yours'll be the same…yeah see, it's different but it's the same. And Steve's… Scott's… How we're going to live, how *long* we're going to live…

STEVEN and SCOTT, easier with each other now they've got SIMON to poke fun at, are looking at their own palms.

SCOTT: Fuck, I'm dead already.

SIMON: I remember I was shitting myself, when that woman started turning my hand like this under the streetlight, looking to see how far my life line went. Jimi was with me.

KARL: Did she read his?

SIMON: Couldn't.

STEVEN: He had gloves on.

SIMON: The lines were too faint...where his lifeline should've been there was just a trickle...fading into his skin...

Beat. SCOTT and STEVEN share a look.

KARL: Are you saying it was fate or something, like he was meant to die?

SIMON: I don't know what it was...it's just...it was in my head. (*Beat.*) Forget it.

Silence.

I could've been a better mate anyway, I can't forget that.

KARL: I know I could.

STEVEN: We all could.

SCOTT: Listen, it's shit what happened to Jimi, but it's not like we have to go round *displaying* how upset we are, it's getting a bit fucking wearing. Let's turn it round, let's celebrate his life. Si, give us another story about Jimi, do one of your dances.

SIMON: What dance?

SCOTT: That jig thing you do, the horny bagpipe
player or something, I don't know.

SIMON: Oh, that!

STEVEN: (*To SCOTT.*) Karl found him.

SCOTT: I know, so let's be honest about it. Karl fucked
up. And at the same time he didn't. Jimi could've
left a message with any of us. He chose Karl, and
that's crap.

KARL: Don't fucking judge me.

SCOTT: I'm not, it's exactly what I'm *not* doing...
You're my mate. I don't know about anyone else,
but I don't blame you for what happened.

STEVEN: *Christ, the arrogance!...* How can you do this;
acting like Jimi's death's got nothing to do with you.

SCOTT: It's to do with all of us.

STEVEN: How long're you keeping this up?

SCOTT: Tell me what 'this' is, yeah? (*Beat. Grabbing his
jacket.*) Anyway, I don't need this crap, maybe it's
better I didn't come in the first place, sorry guys.

SIMON: What's going on with you two?

STEVEN: (*To SIMON.*) Last week, how many times did
you ring him?

SIMON: Forget.

STEVEN: (*To SIMON.*) Blanking you.
Why didn't you return Simon's calls?

SCOTT: Busy.

STEVEN: Busy, or just too upset, too scared to speak to anyone?

SCOTT: How's that then? I spoke to Karl. I can't just get up and leave my job.

STEVEN: They can cope without you.

SCOTT: That's easy for you to say.

STEVEN: So you blank Si, but you speak to Karl when *he* calls. Is it like you mark us out of ten, decide who gets to the top of your list?

SIMON: That's me at the bottom then.

SCOTT: Second from bottom actually.

Beat.

SIMON: You have got a list?

SCOTT: According to Steven, yes.

STEVEN: The point *is...* (*Silence settles.*) Since Jimi died, you've taken a week to get here. If I was in your position I'd drop everything.

SIMON: Well, he's here now, it doesn't matter anymore does it.

STEVEN: Unless I didn't want to come back. Oh okay, maybe nip back for the funeral, get pissed for an hour with my plebby mates and then fuck off back to my flash job, and the blonde I shag on Friday and Saturday nights.

SCOTT: You need to get out more.

SIMON: (*To SCOTT.*) I'm glad you came.

STEVEN: Anything to avoid what really happened; (*Straight at SCOTT.*) or how guilty you feel.

KARL: What's going on?

SCOTT: Fucked if I know.

STEVEN: Tell these two when the last time was that you saw Jimi. (*Beat.*) Tell them why your car was outside Jimi's house the night he died.

Beat.

SCOTT: Is that the trump card you've been dying to play all day?

STEVEN: It's not anything. I'm just… I was dropping by, we knew he was on a downer, so we were taking it in turns to keep an eye on him. I saw your car outside his house, and you haven't mentioned that you were there. Why?

Long silence, until…

SCOTT: (*To KARL.*) Jimi sent you that text, yeah?

KARL nods.

About midnight. Thereabouts, cos I was with him an hour before. (*Still to KARL.*) It was me and you mate; Jimi had a list too. Top four mates; me and you were the top two. Si just not quite making it. Steven? Rock bottom. Sold out.

STEVEN goes for SCOTT, KARL grabs him.

KARL: Calm down...

STEVEN: *Bastard.*

SCOTT: (*Still to KARL.*) I guess Jimi sent the text after I walked out on him. Desperate, or what? But you didn't get it. Was your phone off, or did you just ignore him?

KARL: *It was off.*

SCOTT: Right. So Jimi might still be alive, who knows. You've said it to yourself, how many times have you said it to yourself?

KARL hangs his head.

Long silence.

SIMON: Why didn't you tell us?

STEVEN: That's what I've been wondering.

SCOTT: Do I have to inform you of everything I do?

STEVEN: Were you going to tell Karl?

SCOTT: Why are you doing this?

STEVEN: Because I want you to grieve properly. Something happened...

SCOTT: Yeah?

STEVEN: Yeah. But it's alright.../ whatever it was...

SCOTT: No, you're just out for a bust up because you're... What is it with you? Jesus, *who the fuck are you to decide how people should grieve anyway...*?! I don't...it was just... Me and Jimi...it was something

I didn't expect… I was visiting him, I went to see him because the guy was wearing me down, texting me *all* the time, like he'd latched onto me, like I could sort his life out for him… Alright? *Why?* How could I do that, I'm not a psychiatrist am I, not some fucking… (*Pause.*) So I was just there… To let him down, to tell him I couldn't help him because things've changed… I'm… My life's…

SCOTT stops.

KARL: What did you mean you walked out on him?

SCOTT: What?

KARL: That's what you said.

STEVEN: "I guess Jimi sent the text after I walked out on him. Desperate, or what?"

SCOTT: Is that you taking notes?

SIMON: Why was he desperate?

SCOTT: *Guys…* Jimi was depressed.

STEVEN: Yes.

SCOTT: Exactly. And he's been like it for, how long; what's new?… You just said so yourself (*Puts on his jacket.*) I've had enough.

KARL: Put your fucking jacket down!… (*Beat.*) I need you to tell me. After you'd *been* there he killed himself…so he must've been…what state was he in…how come you weren't worried about him, why didn't you ring any of us…?

Beat.

SCOTT: I don't know.

STEVEN: That's not good enough.

SCOTT: He didn't do it because I walked out.

KARL: But if you'd stayed, then maybe he'd still be alive.

SCOTT: Listen you dozy fucker, I'm not responsible...

KARL: You cheeky fucking...

SIMON: *Karl...*

SCOTT: ...for what someone else does to themselves...

KARL: Wanker.

SIMON: (*To KARL.*) Don't be so hard on him.

SCOTT: Si, I wouldn't waste your breath...he hasn't got a clue what this feels like because he's never got close enough to anyone to find out.

KARL: I got close enough last week though. I was there, and you weren't...or you were, but you just didn't...

SCOTT: What reason would I have had to ring anyone? Since I went away you've all acted like I don't exist.

SIMON: That's just paranoid.

SCOTT: How? Who's been down? Why hasn't anyone been down to stay with me?

STEVEN: It was your choice.

SCOTT: What the fuck does that mean?

STEVEN: That it was your choice to leave. I told you not to.

SCOTT: But can't I move on, can't I get this great fucking opportunity and know that you're all pleased for me...?

SIMON: Look, we'll all come down next week.

STEVEN: This is bullshit.

SCOTT: (*To STEVEN.*) Well I didn't start it.

STEVEN: You're overreacting.

KARL: Just a bit.

SCOTT: *What!*

KARL: I said, just a bit.

SCOTT: Oh yeah, cos Scott's showing his feelings and we can't have any of that. My name's Karl and I don't show my.../

KARL: Yes I / do.

STEVEN: Come on...give it a break for five minutes.

SCOTT: *No!* (*To STEVEN.*) This is what you wanted wasn't it? Fucks' sake... I look at you all and I wonder who's my... Fuck...something happens to me, and you turn it against me, you're pissed off cos I didn't... Look at you... (*He grabs the urn.*) You want to know what was going on with me and Jimi...?... I went to see him cos he'd left me this long rambling indulgent fucked up fucking with my head sort of message, yeah? How he needed just one friend, he had too many friends and one real friend was all he needed, I was strong... I had guts, this is all his words, by the way... So I sat with him for an hour, and he poured his heart out to me. How can people be so... (*Beat.*) he was pathetic...

KARL: Bollocks.

SCOTT: No, he was. And I was pitying him. That's not good. So I... And I'm glad I was there, because I told him he had to jack it in, that I was pissed off with his messages, day and night... I told him to get a grip. When I went for the door he grabbed me by the hand and asked me to stay...(*Pause.*) To lie down with him...(*Beat.*) Hold him while he slept. (*Pause.*) Just that.

Beat.

SIMON: Lie down with him?

SCOTT: Yeah. In his bed.

Beat.

SIMON: Was Jimi gay?

SCOTT: What? *No.* That's not the fucking point is it?

STEVEN: No.

SCOTT: That's what I told myself... It wasn't sex... He just needed... Like he just wanted me to hold him while he was sleeping.

STEVEN: Couldn't you do that?

SCOTT: It wasn't that I didn't want to.

KARL: I would've done it.

SCOTT: You can't say that.

KARL: Yes I can.

SCOTT: *You weren't there.*

KARL: No. But you were.

SCOTT: Yeah, and all the time he's edgy as fuck, I laughed at him...what *was* that?...embarassment, yeah? He started knocking back the vodka...getting irrrational, shouting cos I wasn't doing what he wanted... Jimi was a manipulative bastard, you know what he was like.

KARL: So because you didn't want to be / manipulated you decided you'd......

STEVEN: (*To SCOTT.*) You only had to hold him.

KARL: If it meant/ Jimi stayed alive...

SCOTT: Don't make it sound so easy!! (*To SIMON.*) What would you have done?... Jimi's pissed, he's got a face like...you know...and he wants you to get into bed with him, and hold him while he falls asleep. Do you know what I'm saying? What would you do?

SIMON: Maybe I'd think of something else.

SCOTT: Like what?

SIMON: Erm...

SCOTT: (*To STEVEN.*) How did I know he was going to kill himself...how's it my fault that because I didn't hold him he strung himself up with a fucking rope?

STEVEN: It didn't cross your mind?

SCOTT: Yeah... No... (*Pause.*) I can't change what I felt at the time. On the face of it...it felt weird...to do what he was asking... I...

Long silence. SCOTT picks up the urn.

SIMON: (*Of the urn.*) Be careful with it.

SCOTT: Yeah...(*To KARL.*) Don't want to lose him twice, do we?

KARL goes for SCOTT.

KARL: Bastard...

STEVEN: Karl!

SIMON: Leave him...

KARL grabs at SCOTT, and then goes past him, snatching at the urn and throwing it to the floor. It shatters, the ash flying everywhere. Until...

KARL: ...I was in the kitchen, he was on the stairs. What I can't...*what I can't*...it's in my head...like he knew I'd find him...it's in my head how he knew, and he just...... *I'm* fucking dead, not... Dying. *Me*...that fucker...his...me, *me*...and I'm... (*He stops.*) ... Knew what'd happened...third step...cuppa...(*He looks at his hand, imagining the cup of tea.*)...and he's, hanging... I...tea down, shake, look...wall... carpet...anything to...push...think...push, him, him up, him, and the knot might…legs…holding…noise, low, holding, heavy, always… I'm strongest… stronger than all of you…and he's…and I…where's my will…noise, alive… I keep, I'm holding…he's, him, up, he's…up…heavy…fuck…

Long silence.

SCOTT: …so what else… Does anyone want to start anything else…?

Long silence.

(*To KARL.*) Do you want a beer?

Silence.

Karl.

KARL: (*Quickly.*) No.

Silence.

SCOTT: Well I'm having one. (*Pause.*) I'm having a beer.

But SCOTT doesn't move. Until…

SIMON: Why do men die before women?

Silence.

Because they want to.

STEVEN smirks.

Why did God create man?
Cos vibrators can't mow the lawn.

Silence.

A lobster walks into a bar, and the barman jumps up and says "Oi, you're barred. I'm not having you coming in here giving it all that."

This judge says to Mickey Mouse, "You can't divorce Minnie Mouse because she's got bucked teeth" and Mickey Mouse says, "Your Honour, I didn't say that, I said she's fucking Goofy."

Did you hear about the dyslexic devil worshipper? He sold his soul to Santa.

SIMON continues cracking jokes, and slowly three of them start to climb the ladder. KARL watches them, alone.

End.